[ominous music intensifying]

ALSO BY ALEXANDRA TEAGUE

Nonfiction

Spinning Tea Cups: A Mythical American Memoir

Poetry

Or What We'll Call Desire

The Wise and Foolish Builders

Mortal Geography

Fiction

The Principles Behind Flotation

[ominous music intensifying]

POEMS
ALEXANDRA TEAGUE

A Karen & Michael Braziller Book
Persea Books / New York

Persea Books, Inc.
90 Broad Street
New York, New York 10004

LIBRARY OF CONGRESS CATALOGING-IN-PUBLICATION DATA
Names: Teague, Alexandra, 1974- author.
Title: ominous music intensifying : poems / Alexandra Teague.
    Description: New York : Persea Books, 2024. | "A Karen & Michael Braziller book." | Summary: "Alexandra Teague's fourth collection of poems deepens her ongoing inquiry into American optimism, disillusionment, and violence"—Provided by publisher.
Identifiers: LCCN 2024023713 (print) | LCCN 2024023714 (ebook) |
    ISBN 9780892556069 (paperback) | ISBN 9780892555994 (ebk)
Subjects: LCGFT: Poetry.
Classification: LCC PS3620.E42 O45 2024 (print) | LCC PS3620.E42 (ebook) |
    DDC 811/.6—dc23/eng/20240626
LC record available at https://lccn.loc.gov/2024023713
LC ebook record available at https://lccn.loc.gov/2024023714

Book design and composition by Rita Skingle
Typeset in Elena Basic
Manufactured in the United States of America. Printed on acid-free paper.

ACKNOWLEDGMENTS

Deep thanks to the editors of the following journals for first believing in and publishing these poems, sometimes in earlier versions:

Alaska Quarterly Review, "'The Orange Blossom Special' (arranged for Rome's burning)"

The Arkansas International, "In the Glass Labyrinth at the Nelson Atkins Art Museum, the Rough Beast Is Mistaken for the Minotaur"

Bellingham Review, "[I have had to learn the simplest things last . . .]"

Blackbird, "Lake Chacolet" and "Field Blocks"

Boulevard, "The Rough Beast Listens to a PSA from Lake America"

The Cincinnati Review, "[It is undone business I speak of, this morning]"

Crab Creek Review, "The Rough Beast Receives an Invitation from America"

Four Way Review, "The Rough Beast Would Like the Future To Be Clear"

The Gettysburg Review, "America The Beautiful: Thriftstore" and "Sad Clown Paintings"

The Inlander, "When, Like Garden Spiders from Outer Space, We Return" and "Closed Captions"

The Massachusetts Review, "Crossed Letters from a Concerned American"

Memorious, "The Years I Lived Beneath the Lake"

The Missouri Review, "The Horse That Threw Me"

Northwest Review, "The Rough Beast Goes to Outer Space"

Poetry Northwest, "Mine Eyes Have Seen the Glory"

Puerto del Sol, "The Rough Beast Literally Arrives," "Cambium," "The Goth Comes Clean About Decay"

Southern Humanities Review, "Correlations" (finalist for the Auburn Witness Poetry Prize)

Terrain, "'My Country, 'Tis of Thee' (arranged for Brazen Bull)"; republished in *Dear America: Letters of Hope, Habitat, Defiance, and Democracy*

Water~Stone Review, "The Rough Beast Talks to the Falcon"

Zyzzyva, "The Rough Beast Takes a Painting Class"

Huge thanks to Michael McGriff and Emily Van Kley for insightful, generous comments; to the University of Idaho for a year-long sabbatical; to Cardiff University and its faculty and library for a writing home in Wales; to Gabe Fried, Persea Books, and Civitella Ranieri for a month-long residency where I began "Correlations"; and to Nick Lantz and John Lane for commissioning it as part of Trigger: Artists Respond to Gun Violence. Enduring thanks to my Moscow, Idaho, and inland Pacific Northwest friend and writing community, including Annie Lampman, Laura Read, Kate Lebo, and Maya Jewell Zeller, and my dear colleagues and students at UI, including Jenn Ladino, Tara MacDonald, Erin James, Jodie Nicotra, Leah Hampton, Jess Arndt, Brian Blanchfield, Stacy Isenbarger, Jordan Durham, Wendy Silva, Canese Jarboe, Cady Favazzo, Afton Montgomery, Gianna Stoddard, Libby Croce, Abigail Hansel, Cameron Martin, and Joely Fitch. Thanks to the staff at The Inlander, Sean Hill, and others who asked for work, which I therefore had to write, during the pandemic; to the Port Townsend Writers' Conference for the space and inspiration, and Bruce Beasley for Rough Beast synchronicity; to Elizabeth Bradfield for keen eyes; to Lis McLoughlin and the Writing the Land project and Andrew Armstrong at Taylor Ranch for the week in the wilderness; to my family; to the staff at Persea Books for their ongoing support and care with my words. And to Dylan Champagne for being my first and best reader and helping me keep the faith through all the mean high water.

CONTENTS

[ominous music intensifying]

I

America the Beautiful: Thriftstore

It's not that one person's junk is another's treasure
but that all this junk just *is*.

Like an America that doesn't hide its size-twelve, three-inch heels,
red-glitter-crusted, swaggering even on the holey metal shelf,

but mingles *Learn C++* with light erotica   women in masks
meeting men in masks in castles with masks of fog   where fog is sexy

instead of picnic-pathetic   and no one shivers
because the racks are jammed with coats until the hangers snap   fake-fur-

trimmed collars and hoods fluffed out like Santa dolls suited for an Arctic rave
fuzzy gloves with pom-poms   and pockets with real dimes for free

and ticket stubs to movies that sound like a good idea of your past—
like maybe *that* night got lost when this coat did   and now you have your hands

in its silk lining like you were born here   in this America
where everyone is safe as plastic tumblers and day-glo salad spinners

and no one cares if you walk the aisles in two different shoes like the man
in that children's book with so many caps on caps on caps on his head

you remember no more story but this   like "America the Beautiful"
was only ever purple mountains crayoned so hard the paper wrapping

had to be peeled back   because patriotism meant sacrificing
monarchs and thrones and majesty   and one color to rule them all

because it was always mixed up   what was fantasy and real
and beautiful   and what had to work hard but pretended not to

like the man in the size-twelve heels   calling *Girl, how do these look?*
would never tell you walking in this country is free

but walks on anyway   the kitchenware aisle a runway
spice racks and cutting boards painted with tiny amber waves of grain

so it's not true you only remember purple   there are shining seas
and fruited plains on cups everyone's grandmother died to leave here

the past reflecting back into now in a closet mirror bungeed to the racks
and the purses empty of everyone's fear of losing—

that majesty of the already-gone but refillable   like a bin of hats
which maybe *was* the whole story   how the man carried

all of them with him   like a country that erects monuments
not only for presidents but also for this-man-was-lynched-here-

and-now-there's-a-swingset   the true story
of every broken thing until now   and someone paying at the register

for a bag of it   and no one saying
blue tags can't be 50 percent off   and no one driving in in a Hummer

and no one saying braided straps on purses are passé
or torn-cover paperbacks are not a type of sock   some Sunday

no one noticing you rummaging in the evening gowns' dust ruffles
for what you can't believe is but is this pair of heels

the Statue of Liberty floating in each plastic wedge   cloudy glitter
raining around her island when you shake them   when you step into them

strap the coral plastic straps   America in exactly your size   and how, girl,
did you ever walk before this?   She has a tiny torch   she's calling everyone

no matter how tired or poor   between the linoleum
and your purple-painted toenails   to just go ahead and rise.

"Orange Blossom Special" (arranged for Rome's burning)

I want you to hear the first notes when the fiddle
starts to sound like a train, though even then there's something
squawky to it, something donkey about the wheels

along the high thin trestle of the strings, though maybe
the bow is the trestle and the fiddle is the train upside down
in the dark of the tunnel, which is also the audience:

I want you to hear people in an Ozark theater clapping harder
as it bears down at them and the pink gel lights keep blooming,
and the woman dueling now with the man in the red silk vest

keeps carrying on, which is what we mean by a showstopper:
that it barrels toward us, screeching of wheels turning
in the air by her shoulder, her chin cupping a freight train

that must be a passenger train, aren't we all on it?
The fiddles fiddling as Rome, well you know what it does,
but it looks less like flames and more like sunset or Fire

in the Hole, a rollercoaster that dived in the dark in a mine
that was just a building built to look old-timey—thin plastic
fringe with orange lights shining behind, the pumped-in sound

of crackling. Hands in the air for a mine fire. Hands in the air
for the Bald Knobbers with their black-horned masks and cut-
out eye holes, who set the fire, who no one mentioned, helped set

the Ozarks on the tracks of whiteness. Hands in the air for
a family ride based on vigilantes, for a past that people
(some people) plunge into and come out laughing. It's what

the music of this country rushes from and keeps on playing:
one long track for a luxury liner called *The Orange Blossom
Special* that sped to Florida in the 1940s as white people

slept under white sheets like orange petals drifted from
groves to the sound of that rocking that's the sound of
this fiddling as the strings keep burning, as the fiddlers smile

in satiny ruffles. Didn't they back up the Nashville greats?
The program says so. The program's full of the near-adjacents.
Hands on its glossy paper if they might be your ancestors

who played on as the country burned and lights that said
Country burned, meaning something different or else the same
in a box called *entertainment*. Hands in the air if you grew up

near here, if you loved the magic shows, where tigers disappeared
from their cages and came back roaring. Hands in the air
if you fear the air here; if the stage has trapdoors; if the train

has trapdoors; if the fiddle keeps barreling; if the song's
familiar as it flattens you, as it whistles by you, as it does not
flatten you; if you know that dilemma of the trolley lever

that's really a train lever: whom do you save? Hands in the air
if it's not your choice. If it is your choice. If the trolley's
automated. If you're being held up; if the music keeps coming;

if the clapping's going to start now; if you don't want to hear
the foot stomp and popcorn rattle in this icebox theater; if
you're not immune to it; if you fear your own blood that ran

through your grandmother and her real father who beat his
wife back in West Virginia stone-cold dead, like they say,
though the body's not stone; it's more like a horse

before it turns into the hairs of a fiddle bow. Hands in the air
if there's blood all over them. If there's blood on his knuckles
in the gas station bathroom as he drives to Texas to fuck

his lover, so nine months later: your grandmother. Hands
in the air if the show is over; if the show's just starting; if
the parking lot lights keep fritzing like bug zappers; if no

one in your family's ever been to Rome, just the Olive
Garden in Paris, Texas. Hands in the air if you'd like more
breadsticks. If Rome's being redlined. If this ride's

too violent. If you'd like to ask the dead some questions. If
you can hardly hear yourself. If the train that's not a train
is screeching closer, whistling and wheedling as the emcee's

saying *Wow, folks! Have you ever heard a fiddle sound like that?*
Did a train just go right through our hearts, or what? Well, give it up!

The Horse That Threw Me

It's not about climbing back on the horse after the horse
has thrown you if the horse has thrown itself inside you:
the spooked song of bone, the shadow whip. If no
lawn will ever again be free of corners you cannot turn
your head past: periphery of acorn and cedars, long gold
breath of the grass outside the barn: a grave in the field
light leaks through. You will pass to your death again
and again like this: still living as part of you clenches
like a saddle buckle, clinks against itself. What a tangle
of *for* and *into* to explain why you loved *Equus* in college
and would not trail-ride the migraine-bright spring fields.
Didn't you want to canter beyond yourself? Of course you
did. Didn't you want to be a centaur made of two whole
animals, not pain and its absence? Some days, nothing
breathes down your neck. The barbed-wire fences are
bare, untufted by horsehair. On the free, green lawn,
only the wind tosses its head and whinnies. You hold
out your hand to it. Appleless girl with an unreadable
future, you could be anyone, your body well enough
to forget. But here the real past catches you, or you
step toward it: the dark wild eyes of it. The musky air.
Wherever the lines of you lead, they'll circle back:
a song sung as a round: that girl riding a crocodile
your third-grade teacher loved: *She sailed away on a
happy summer day on the back of a crocodile . . . At the end
of the ride, the lady was inside. And the smile was on*
. . . What a simple tangle irony seems to a child. Again
and again, you'll pass through your life like this: uneaten,
unable to say when what you thought you were riding
toward your future became the past that rides you.

The Rough Beast Listens to a PSA from Lake America

Down in the deep blue waters
of America, where submarines
practiced their sonar, there is no
creature. We repeat, there is no
creature rising. Beneath the pressure-
treated lumber of new docks,
the mosquito-swarm whirring
of waterskiers, the spit-static speakers
of the boats blaring past with glittered
hulls, only the light shines: thin
as the glaze on breakfast pastries;
the McDonald's gold and cheerful
beaks of swans. Their bodies have
been hollowed to hold families
on bench seats with two sets of peddles
for circling and circling. Unroyal thrones
with backswept feathers like Elvis's
pompadour gone patriotic white.
The day is exactly the size of this.
Leak proof. Cooler-zipped. The lake
is the size the Freedom Dam made it.
It is made of its surface.
It is made of Lee Greenwood
crackling in ripples of passing wake:
I'd thank my lucky
stars to be
livin' here today
though (we repeat),
no one lives here.
The turbines are the restlessness
you're hearing. There is no creature
churning in the mud-flapped depths.
Nothing but the swans arch
their necks. They are rentable

hourly. Safe for children
as far as the buoys.
There is no lifeguard
on duty. No woman sweeping
up bubbles and perch from
her long-drowned porch.
The people were paid
to move away from the town
that was flooded. Their
mailboxes rust now: the long
swinging arms for when
the snow plows struck them,
algaed and silt-slunk.
Snow melts in the lake now.
Snow melts into summer.
We repeat: no one is looking up
through a thousand feet of water,
missing the starlight. The boats
are private, safer stormclouds
And the flag
still stands for freedom
crackling across the flat full sky of lake.
It is the afterlife of river.
It is freedom secured
and spillwayed. God's voice
booming back louder
from the high flat concrete
of the temple wall. There is no God
before or beneath this.
There is no creature
you cannot proudly fish for.
You can peddle in circles,
or you can peddle harder; you can
rent a better swan.

We are not responsible if you
drown—now that we've told you
there is no way to
(we repeat). Nothing
to drag you down.

Mine Eyes Have Seen the Glory

Admitting, I've never stopped wanting
the misheard line—*my knives*—those blades
graced with handles and sight. About glory:
who knew anything in kindergarten? At best, a plastic bucket
of chlorine water dumped over my head: apocalyptic
(I didn't know the word yet) and baptismal. Atheist
child: this was the closest I would get. Pool tiles in cool
Texas morning: the swim teacher shocking us into submission,
bravery, freedom, glory: whole countries
of abstraction I only saw with mine eyes wringing, whinging, stinging
water. I mean, with my body and its sudden
blindness in the face of.
About this country: who gets to dive and rise
and who gets trampled like the vintage, I still can't see
the justice at forty-three. Madmen keep singing on TV: *It's all an act;*
those children never died for real. New mouths keep
mouthing: *We're praying for the victims' families. We are*
praying . . . This is freedom. We used to sing,
facing the flag like it could hear us. We used to sing
His truth is marching. We once held ice cubes shaped
like Texas in a Texas schoolroom
where no one shot us. Just water dripping from our fingers. Glory
glory to the playground
hippopotamus with its rusting springs
we bounced on. Glory to the air a child leaves
and then returns to: mine knives have seen
the pool headfirst: the concrete, the drain's dark suction, but then
the bubbling back, sweet surface breaking. Hallelujah
to the desks shaped like desks
a child has no reason to dive beneath: the fiery
gospels of cinnamon jolly ranchers, the trumpets of ice cream cones,
then Texas melting down to clean our fingers. About naivety
and 1980: we were all mid-air, headlong,
this country heading where it's gone
(as the saying goes): *If we don't change direction . . .*

My jubilant feet above my head—*with you my grace shall deal*—
as I hit the pool water. *Let us die. Let us die.* Let us dive
to make men free. We used to sing upside down. We used to
face the flag like it could see us
as we *builded Him an altar.* As He sifted our hearts
like playground sand into a bucket. (We never asked what if He
or he or he *loosed the fateful lightning*; there were sides
straight as stripes on the flag; we were the future
sang Whitney Houston. We were the world, sang Michael Jackson.)
If our eyes got rusty, someone—glory glory—
would polish them, wouldn't they?, until we reflected stars.

The Rough Beast Receives an Invitation from America

Come as you are; come
with your fur crushed smooth
as applesauce from a blender. Come
as a 1950s housewife, Maytag-tested
version of yourself. Bleach your blood
of stains of place and dust. Come like wine
without terroir. All terror of specificity removed—
claws and wings and slouch and sluff and
dandruff shampooed off. Be hateable only
because you're beautiful. Come with knees unbent,
your flag pin pinned, your beast eyes focused
on the ball. Don't cheat by asking us what game.
Catch or be caught. Come half-mast as a school flag
in the aftermath. It's called respect.
Come TSA-approved, pre-checked. All contamination
sealed in one-quart bags. Put your dirty paws
above your head. Be the fears that we expect. Dark
shadows in city streets. Foreclosed windows. Meth.
Roaring lions at the Manhattan, Kansas, safari park.
Come from the desert we made for you.
Come like sand in an hour glass. We decide
when to turn it. We decide how to mount
your head on the ski lodge wall. Don't come bird-
spiraled, stalking, though that's how we'll tell it. How
dangerous. How wild. How vermin, how refugee.
Come without concupiscence or too many
strange syllables. Come with sins we recognize
from Bible school; blur out the rest like breasts:
skin-colored wasps swarming parts we shouldn't see.
Come as the tower poet couldn't dream you. As 3D,
as bit-coin, as the VR ride that spins us in its wide
widening gyre. Let us scream but don't kill us.
Come as Ruff Beast and rap for us. Come
like the unborn with perfect blue passports.
Come worship at our megachurch. Come like

wrapping paper from Amazon. Like a re-run
of Tarzan. Like subwoofer to the loud-
thumping heartland. When we say *Rough Beast*,
you say *America.* When we say *holes*, we mean
assholes and *pussies* and *mouths* and *prisons*, and
round glazed balls of donut: a hole's sweet
opposite. Come. There's nothing but center here.

Correlations

I.   On a graph I loved to understand in junior high,
           each July, people seemed to drown because of ice cream—
           lakewater rippled with their bodies, wet sugar
           crystalling the life ring, the lifeguard licking
           the deep-end blue of a coconut popsicle, dreaming

as a boy waves—heat spike & sweet spike & splash of a body
creamed, as we used to say then: *man, he creamed you*
in that race; she creamed you at that free throw; I creamed the test
after I learned that two lines can climb a single curve

     sly & steady as the morning heat,
                       without causation:
     motorcycle wrecks & cheese; steak dinners & the gristle
     of lightning strikes; golf-course profits & Nicholas Cage;
     spilled Diet Coke & bodies on the floor after *The Dark Knight Rises;*

or in the further future, after that pool party where the man
dials his phone (*it is apparent [he] wanted his girlfriend to listen in*), then
fires into the rubber backs of deck chairs, & then & then &
then & then & then & then & then

II.   It's so easy, you can do it yourself, on the back
           of a napkin, BJ Campbell writes. He's out to prove
           everyone's lying about the link between gun ownership and
           homicides. He excludes the data-skewing stats
           of suicide, police violence, accidents. Marks each
           state's guns & homicides as little dots. You'll see,
           he says, there's absolutely no way you could draw
           a line for any correlation; it's far too scattered,
           like someone shot a piece of graph paper with #8 birdshot.

III.   Arkansas, where I was raised in heat that drove us to double-
dip ice cream cones for tourists, dip ourselves in motel pools—
sneaking through flimsy gates to their splotch-&-foot-scald
edges—ranks #5 out of all the states for gun deaths.

Coincidental
to a July 4 on which at least six people were shot in the Little Rock area
comes . . . a survey that shows Arkansas No. 2 among the states
in the percentage of adults who own guns.

Coincidental,
which meant originally, *to fall upon together.*

IV.   The man who wanted his girlfriend to listen to him, listen
to him, held a cell phone that killed no one by a pool chair

that killed no one, by stripey towels & sun-
screen, pool noodles, paddleboards

too small to be gurneys. You could make a dot for each item
on a paper napkin. You could look away

at confounding factors. Mental health. Video games.
Freedom. You could draw dots until they cluster like stars

on the flag for an impossible country
that hasn't heard of constellations. Pool towel. Pool noodle.

A history of rage & isolation. Some people are just lonely. You can pile
Dippin' Dots at the ball park, at Worlds of Fun—

cream plus liquid nitrogen—ice cream made into
individualism. There's no winged horse in the sky; no dipper

but this metal in a teenage hand. You can wipe
your mouth on the napkin, say *doesn't always equal*

means *never equals.* You can forget cigarettes & lung cancer,
air bags & seat belts & survival in collisions. Before

an American invented it, who ever dreamed
of beaded ice cream? Who imagined hate on a sunny day?

V.   In the duke's palace in Urbino, Italy, sculpted
into the door lintels (his guestrooms, his parlor,
his own wife's bedroom) acorn-shaped jellyfish
dangle plaster tentacles—tidal & poisonous
& painted gold. Their flamelike drift
inexplicable in inland Umbria
until the art historian explains they aren't *ulmaridae* at all,
but early Renaissance grenades: petards in mid-explosion
like tentacled rocket ships. Federico's motto,
Ich Kann Verdauen Ein Grosses Eisen:
I can swallow a big iron, reboasted in their vaulting
each door each guest had to pass through,
(the non-ornamental ornaments of power
impressing that even he, humanist, philanthropist, was a force
not to fuck with). Their high-tech threats
floating through dreams, streaming like *rampage & carnage*
& America's deadliest summer on record, which finds me even here
this summer, which *is ending as it began . . . this month's loss of life*
most acute in Texas—acute, which no longer & maybe never meant
the opposite of *chronic,* but something like terror
becoming ever young again. Becoming near
transparent & proliferate as moon jellies
I thought once, swimming off the coast, were innocent,
like living soap bubbles
until a single tendril slipped across my lip.

VI.   And if there is a reason, the preachers say, it is God
exiled from the school; God
who wants to sit at his swiveling
chair-desk as the bell buzzes, as the teacher flips the lights
on like the fourth day. God
who wants standardized tests
& pink erasers & the hearts of each American. Twizzlers & tater tots &
obeyance of metal detectors inside &
outside the heart. God who wants social science & civics
classes on the 2nd Amendment He gave this country
to save its people from Tom-Petty freefalling—
people with their souls mixed up like pop rocks & spit, that crackling
on the tongue, those sinners who never learned to call God's name
like a roll call, never asked for Him
to sit beside them in Earth Science
after He created this very Earth,
never bowed their heads or bubbled in the True-Right answers
of *a) God b) God c) More God*
d) Damn the rest; the preachers say,
if teenagers are dead again in a school today
it's *for the root cause of Godless, depraved* hearts,
this country's impenitent desks, the simple subtraction
of opening to Chapter 5, when God wants
His own words to crack the spine
of every morning. *Let every patriotic American*
have the right to hold a gun, God says,
& they do. *Let me use my big pink eraser to rub out danger,* God says,
or He could have.

VII.   *The preamble thus both sets forth the object of the Amendment*
and informs the meaning of the remainder of its text . . .
'it cannot be presumed that any clause in the constitution
is intended to be without effect'
                      from the dissenting opinion in *District of Columbia v. Heller*

A well-regulated militia being necessary to the security
of the sweatpant racks at Walmart, to a festival
of artichokes & fresh-fried garlic, to a man sloshing
a Manhattan under dance-floor strobes, to a bank lobby,
a synagogue, a pool party, a bipolar man in his room alone; a well-
regulated militia being necessary to each individual
knuckle on the man's fist knocking against another man's
windshield at the Stinker Station by the hardware store
where the LED sign flashes ads for *Festival Dance* at the university,
the parking-lot *Gem Show*, their own *Enhanced Conceal-Carry* class;
a well-regulated militia being necessary to the fingers &
whole bald palm of that hand now covering the glass,
his face leaning in to shout, *go back where you came from, N--.*
If I was carrying this morning, I'd shoot you. A well-regulated militia
being absent, my friend, a colleague of that *you*, calls the police,
says, *he was on his way back-to-school shopping; his daughter*
was in the car; he's Pakistani; he was scared to call. A well-regulated
teacher / first-responder being necessary for the free State's
classrooms where they teach, where I teach, three miles across the state line,
but still in America, we know about absolute clauses
& causation: *Speed being necessary to stop someone from bleeding to death,*
your shirt, paper towels, Kleenex, whatever you have
can be used to staunch the blood flow. Or, *a well-regulated*
Back-to-School list being necessary
to succeed in third grade, which does not mean, and is never
made to mean that we *each* need small plastic protractors
& lunch boxes & Hello Kitty erasers—
although my younger cousins' list in rural Texas
includes laminated name tags on lanyards
they have to wear daily now, they tell me, in case
a well-regulated body count is necessary.

VIII.   I was raised in Arkansas in a family-that-did-not-own-guns
        that owned a gun. My mother kept it in her dresser drawer
        wrapped in a scarf like the one she wore rare days she pinned
        her hair in auburn knots. Those latent curls. Latent shimmer
        of its mother-of-pearl stock in the winter-shirt-wooled dark
        as she & I fought & cried, as my boyfriend / foster brother
        punched himself square in his eye—those rings of purple-black
        like a wayward planet. He hadn't been diagnosed yet. We never
        said bipolar also ran in our family. I gave a speech as valedictorian:
        Progress lies not in enhancing what is, but advancing toward what will be
        with him, swollen-eyed behind me, my own bruised ribs forgotten
        before they even happened. *Latent*, from *ladh, hidden*, relative of *lethe*,
        the river we swam, forgetting the bullets, the nylon scarf,
        the hurt we were capable of

IX.   The effects of human voices on other animals—
        even ones we think of as predators, even the mountain
        lions which grow skittish, avoid the trails

        if NPR plays from speakers, or a woman's voice
        in *genteel tones* recites a poem—is what ecologists call
        the landscape of fear, which sounds like a metal band

        that senior in Algebra who pressured & flirted with me
        to borrow my bracelet for *just one day*, then gave
        it to his girlfriend, would have loved; like that nightfall

        on an Oakland street three men crossed quick from
        different corners, converging toward me—that run-down
        store I ducked into, & them through the window & me

        pretending I needed *Snickers or Ruffles or Ruffles or anything*—
        that old fear-song of *why were you ever here? where
        can you go now at night in America?* That landscape

of gunshots we'd hear sometimes bedtimes, saying
"maybe fireworks?" near no known holiday.
Unclasped fear in our backs after each new headline

when we'd all guard our bodies, keep *our distance from
the grids, move cautiously along a mental map of risk.*
Those men's still-there laughter, those men with bullets

at their backs too in this racist country. We learn to
detour. We *human super predators,* our softest voices
reading *The Wind in the Willows, profoundly disturbing*

the animals, so the raccoons stop eating, so fish
proliferate, then mussels, whole cascades.

X.   Though it's known to contain as much radiation as a
       collapsing star, no one knows for sure if dark lightning has
       ever struck a person. Invisibility makes correlation hard to
       prove. When my nephew shot himself, a man in their ghost
       town (*diminished mining town,* my sister calls it) used dowsing
       rods to find space in the old-West cemetery. *There are so
       many unmarked bodies,* he told us, *best not just start digging.* He
       showed us after: the rods held loosely in his hands like reins
       of an invisible horse. He'd learned from his father, witching
       for water. To explain plot, teachers say, *if a gun is introduced
       on page two, it has to be fired by the end.* Because I didn't know
       my nephew had a gun, I didn't think, *a gun means he's three
       times more likely to die by suicide.* I found that out later in the
       story. *There was no life you could live out to its end,* says a poem
       he loved. Studies show dowsing is no more accurate than
       chance: the person reads the landscape's cues, hands moving
       before the rods do. When people say, *Guns don't kill people,
       people kill people* they mean *if people are introduced on page two.*
       Because beef consumption doesn't correlate with lightning

in one famous graph doesn't negate all correlations. When my sister called, dark lightning struck through my phone. At almost 26, Gabriel was my youngest nephew. My family prides itself on precision. In 2016, 22,000 people holding a gun died in America. *Ghost town is inaccurate. It's never been fully uninhabited*, my sister says. Dowsing rods don't bury people, people bury their friend's son with dowsing rods. The man was backhoeing a deep, perfect rectangle when we arrived. He climbed down to show us how he'd found the site with a mountain view. He held out two thin metal L-shaped rods. We looked where they pointed, though we knew.

Sad Clown Paintings

for Chad

A painter friend has developed a theory:
everything is a sad clown painting, but only sad clown
paintings know this—which makes a serious, squeaking,
twisted balloon-animal sense as the Air Quality Map burns
burgundy *Hazard* for weeks of wildfire, the sky a depthless
silted grey as if a child with ten thumbs has fingerpainted
the swirls each of us sad-clown stands in, or like a madman
with orange hair has dried his sticky hands on the towel
of other people's lives, as Houston sinks, and Mumbai sinks
and the tiny blimp of news floats across my screen: Oaxaca, Mexico,
where I lived one summer of old-fashioned sky, is rubbled
zocalos of rebar and concrete; all the bad news simultaneous
like those big white clown lips are also the deflated rubber
of the balloon the clown had dreamed of blowing into something
beautiful. Or as Alexis de Tocqueville said, *In a revolution, like a novel,*
the most difficult part to invent is the end because he couldn't imagine
chat rooms: how wind farms will kill us; how cloned sheep will
save us; if Taylor Swift really hid her boob job; *Who is the artist?*
Does it have distinctive features? Are you sure it's a clown? Although
he also wrote, *History is a gallery of pictures in which there are few originals*
and many copies. Where we all prepare faces to meet the faces
that we meet. Red noses and greasepaint warning, *Don't you remember*
Nero? What did you think all those fiddles meant? As our carnival rides
keep *mad-dogging their tilta whirls*, as Tom Waits, in his saddest of all
sad-clown voices would sing, and a hurricane 400-miles wide
is barreling at Cuba, at Florida, and we should all call our senators
about the EPA/everything, but I stutter on telephones; I'd rather
talk in person; I want to fly to see the Northern Lights; to float
on a lake on a rubber raft blown into the shape of penguin; and
It's slow work, because of all the gauzy light, it's hard to pick out anything—
like my favorite poet, who became an addict, said of the *apocalypse—*
which all my friends are calling this; their rueful, joking tones

like bows tied loosely over sadness, like *every generation thinks it's bad,*
but what if our hair in this country can only be on fire for so many centuries?
What if all the flowers, bees, birds really fade into black, and in the final
spotlight is just an old felt hat, blubbery lips, and those eyes staring
down and out, and down and out, like the world is a literal pun, or a cliché—
that part about *all the world's a clown,* or is it *loves one?*

Crossed Letters from a Concerned American

More young people believe they'll see a U.F.O. than that they'll see their own
Social Security benefits.
        —*Mitch McConnell*

Dear M—

It's true that once I took a ferry across the Balearic Sea to Ibiza to dance
all night like an alien that hasn't heard of sleep. I had glowstick eyes
and a red string bikini, which sounds glamorous, like fire ants
sound exotic on a sandwich if you've never had a picnic; I mean I
had razor-stubbled legs and A-cup breasts and felt lonely
for Earth while I was on Earth. I was, like many Americans, a human
girl. I wanted music so loud it vibrated my bones into string theory.
I mean, I wanted answers to questions of the universe I didn't understand.
I understood the question shouldn't be only money or men who pilfered
it grain by grain from the beaches where I dug my toes. I understood foam
refusing containment by shape-shifting. It's true I wanted to feel at home
like that, which is maybe how I was most humanly alien. What if
you'd been there that night, when they flooded the dance floor's straws
and Solo cups and shoes and all, and pumped in those bubbles? The raw

                                                           → *sideways*

light of strobes raking and raking over everything like a drunk Zen
garden. We were drifting stones then. We were dancing in mop water.
I imagine this is how you imagine me: in some slick concavity called *Sin:*
El Pecado, Los Pecadillos, the little sinful disappointments as the party after
that cheesy EDM, that sloshing dancefloor, the DJs loudly phoning it in,
foaming it in. What I mean is you would not be wrong, and neither
would I for being there. For being, as you said Americans are, *too speedy.*
Young people don't have to believe in UFOs to take the moon personally,
or to understand those scenes in B movies where the alien rushes
toward a human body and becomes it, like the moment strangers
in train stations become most real as they hug whoever they came for.
Sometimes I imagine you will peel off your human face to reveal only dust.

Sometimes, that you'll slip off your strange suit of hatred to show
the soft pulsing heart of you, waving like a moon jelly in a shower of cold

→ *vertical*

fire-sprinkler rain as the dj says to. I know I paid too much for what
someone else sold me as magical. I tried to escape commodification
in a bikini and a tiny dress. When the music turned off so late it was also light
out, I walked to the beach that had been there blocks away, washing in
all along, wave after foaming wave; waded in in my wet clothes like a stray
fish or a heroine of a Victorian novella. But I didn't hate or love the world
enough to leave it. I floated in it, like most of us. And yes, the great grey
machines of capitalism and pain kept churning; yes, missiles in the holds
of ordinary-seeming planes kept flying over. What I mean is I know I closed
my eyes. I treaded water that was only sometimes even real water. I felt
like the party bus driving through red lights: I might confuse the intersections
of myself with everything: buoys, boys, a cruise ship's wake, the yellow quilt
of the horizon. I wanted to. What I mean is, even as a child, I thought men
with metal detectors must be aliens. Who else would listen to their own

→ *sideways*

beeping stick for hints of coins when the duck pond was an iridescent mess
of paddling and honking, or shells zithered and shifted as the waves washed in?
What I mean is, there's a whole damn beautiful ocean out there, Mitch,
and it seems like all you love are symbols. Like crop circles and babies
on billboards and huge white crosses: things that stay in their fields or
fields you've stuck them in. Once I had to explain to a man who'd moved
to Arkansas for me that the people lugging a giant cross down the shoulder
of the highway weren't going to crucify anyone. I was raised there so it made
sort-of-sense to me, like the Fun Spot waterslide with its rough blue concrete
and suit-snagging trickle made sense because it was the only waterslide
for counties. As a Californian, he couldn't see why people would carry
faith big enough to kill a man. He was frightened of them. In *Arrival*,
that movie with squid-like aliens, the symbol those aliens draw is three-
dimensional, but if you don't know this, *tool* can get misread as *weapon*;

→ *vertically*

I don't think you care if people confuse those. I don't think you want
what I think of as safety. What I mean is, we need more dimensions
to understand each other. Or maybe we need smaller symbols. Or a slant
that lets us read more words so nothing cancels out—like those old cross-
hatched letters from the 19th-century. Paper and postage were costly
then; words had to fit both ways on single pages. What I mean is, flag
stripes one way could mean *I pledge allegiance to kneeling out of hope and grief.*
And stripes the other way: *I pledge allegiance to what I believe is God rippling*
above this country. Like that chewing gum ad from my childhood—*double your*
pleasure, double your fun—which I admit sounds less like mint and more
like a threesome when I say it now. What I mean is, this country is bigger
than we're making it—like those sci-fi movies that waste the vast frontiers
of space on a plot that orbits only the lead man's daddy issues. Or squid
scribing of distant galaxies, but we only hear the story we arrived with:

→ *over (and over)*

white-mother-and-baby on a loop of time, like an old-fashioned slide
projector. In the 80s, two vegetarian hippy pacifist atheists who believed
in Reagan's fiscal conservatism and movie-star starlight, took me,
their daughter, to a meeting of people in the Ozarks. Clandestine
CIA helicopters were smuggling shipments of cocaine at night
in neighboring pastures. The slides lifted and fell with that tick-
clunk like a conspiracy metronome. There were crops blighted
by propeller winds; scraped-mud landings. We were supposed to listen
for rumbles in the air between whippoorwills: the way power had decided
to use us for its secret ends. What I mean is, we all want our fields' bent
stalks to mean something. We all go swimming in moonlight
that's really a cow pond: that clay-suck-and-cow-shit squelching the slits
between our toes like we're a creature evolving from webbed feet
or back again; duckweed gritty on our t-shirts because the August heat

→*sideways*

of our own fears has become unbearable. Or at least I once did
this as a teenager. It's so hard not to project ourselves. To let the sky
not be just a bigger planetarium. Someone with a laser dot that drifts
like a satellite along Orion's belt to show us how star buckles to starlight,
like those ruled Big Chief pads where I learned to make my name the size
it was supposed to be. I think we should admit we've pulped history
into paper. We should talk about the feather headdress's dime-
store stereotype, the carved-wood man outside my hometown's old-time
portrait studio, where tourists could play dress up by an out-of-tune piano
as silk-vested gangsters and innocent prostitutes. We could try to know
more of history's sour notes, and care less about permanence: the kind
where white people pose like ghosts of everyone. In H.G. Wells' sci-fi,
the Victorian aliens have stiff insect bodies and eyes like prison teardrops,
and the moon's deeply hollow. And sometimes I think America is its giftshop,

→ vertically

hung with solar-wind windchimes and gold-plated moon cheese
you only get if you were born on a spaceship. I mean, we seem
confused about upward mobility and gravity. We keep peeling away scars
over band-aids marked *Pull Yourself Up By Your Bootstraps; American
Exceptionalism; Freedom's Not Open for Questions*. Mitch, you say you're a man
who sleeps easily, and I believe you—the way my friend's father in his car
fell asleep at the wheel and drove off the street into a stranger's house,
right through their living room. What's the purpose of laws after laws
about walls if you're crushing our couches? Sometimes America strikes
me as a thriftstore game box with two Yahtzee die, some blue and green
bills from Monopoly, and those little plastic battleships; the rules MIA,
though one kid keeps announcing he's won the railroad-large-straight-
destroyer. Like the boy in my class with *He Who Dies With The Most Toys Wins*
on his favorite t-shirt, which even then, in fifth grade, made me squirm

→ sideways

at how *Dies* was not the verb I was supposed to care about. I mean I think
we need to go back and diagram our own most basic propositions.
With Liberty and Justice for All might, like that famous *Princess Bride* line,
not mean what you think it means. Or if you *do* mean AR15s, chainlink,
and backroom abortions, then you need to talk about all the *bloodstain,*
bloodsport, bloodspot, bloodthirsty entries you've left out of the dictionary.
In H.G. Wells' *The First Men In the Moon,* one man in the rocket's rickety
metal ball, like a Victorian tea strainer gone galactic, keeps insisting he should
be the boss of the cricket-like moonbeings, though he has no way to survive
in their atmosphere; he's crashed uninvited, armed only with reason, self,
stale parataxis like *I came; I saw; I conquered. I saw* as that small lettuce fluff
in a sandwich of *I'm Here to Kill You.* We could use our human eyes
for more than this; we could practice those trust-building games where you
can't look away from some stranger until you think they are actually you

→ *over*

in different skin, or you're madly in love with them, or you're full of fear
of the ways we all hold strange dark moon caverns we won't let anyone
into. Once, my father, a former journalist, attended an Arkansas small-town
UFO conference. He filled a Steno pad with drawings of fields of crops sheared
to circles that meant, in different ways, *we are here, Horatio, beyond the heaven*
and earth you've dreamt of. (CIA aside, he was usually less moved by conspiracies
than Shakespeare.) He showed us page after page of those intricate geometries
of contact. It was years before I knew he'd been struggling then with his own
sexuality. In the song "America" by Simon and Garfunkel, they say *We've all gone*
to look for America, or that's how I remember it, though it's really *They've all come*
to look for America, and that means *us,* not aliens, but us searching everywhere for
where we are. I mean, it's humbling to be lost in your own country, Mitch.
I mean, I'm scared for this country. I think we need a map that's big
enough for contradictions; I think we're seeing the directions wrong,

→ *vertically*

or looking in too few. We're talking stock markets versus aliens when
what we need is fields of real living corn with beautiful, strange tassels.
Sometimes, your face reminds me of that man at the post office in Oakland
who worked the counter and hated letters or stamps or people or postal
scales, or all of these. He wanted us to feel ashamed and small. Once he yelled,
You're not allowed to mail so much air! because I had five poems with a self-
addressed-stamped envelope folded inside an envelope that was over-full
like naïve hope or a time capsule. I tried to argue air's weightlessness,
but he glared, waving my #10 self-adhesive sin at me. If someone was cross
for no reason, my mother used to say, "Just imagine, probably her shoes
are hurting her." I'm writing about your feet, Mitch. Would you like to sit?
Has the leather been pinching? What if you stop measuring my envelope, then
simply breathe? Did you see they've just found water on the moon? I mean
we could surprise ourselves still. How is it, really, over there in your human skin?

II

[It is undone business I speak of, this morning]

After the corner where the white dog with the flat
shark head at the head-high fence, and the hill's burst

of planter-box vines and trampolines, the water tower
holds its steel cloud of lake. What pumps must it use;

what ordinary spells against gravity. The father spreading
paper-doll-collapsing boxes of McDonalds for his son

in its picnic-tabled shade, emptying them into the empty
green of summer day. What ordinary optimism: one-way

suck of straw between mouth and world; the tower's
legs lifting always upward. What belief in my own legs

as unsurprisingly alive that keeps me running on, not
pooling on the lawn until my parents drive out of the past

to find me—roll down the station wagon's windows
to let luck in; wasp on the dashboard; seat belts clanking.

What safety of that nylon belt, those seconds as
my father braked behind the flatbed braking at the light,

steel pipes shearing off it down our station wagon's side,
chalkboard-metal screech of doors from hinges. What

fourth wall opening. The road where it had always been:
leg-length away. What belief that ever learns again to say

inside and outside will hold their place? Low chainlink of yard
dog head. French fries spilling from their sun-spot carton.

What valves that keep the water in the sky until it's time
to drink it. What pipes arrowing. Oil, drainage, metal, car

tin-canning open; here-is-the-churching open like a child's
hands. What ordinary child hasn't played *Here is the steeple*;

open the door, turning the rafters inside-out to praying
people. What kind of safety, breaking apart to make us?

"My Country, 'Tis of Thee" (arranged for Brazen Bull)

a Greek device used to torture . . . the Brazen Bull
had an acoustic setup that converted human screams into
the sound of a bull . . . [through] a complex system of tubes and stops
*   —Medieval Chronicles*

Bellow and bellicose   and the men   and the man's crying
on the stand   red-faced arrogant even in distress   are furnacing
hot new foundries in the news   melting the metals they have
always melted   and women are singing in the burning bronze
and also and also me and the time I was six   and twenty and twelve and forty
and I believe   and of thee I sing   of the scared-into and the clamped-quiet
woods of shame   bottle shatter and condoms'   spent fireworks'
rocket-red glare in another song   that is not the song the women
sing in the key of keys-spiked-from-fists for the last three blocks   and the dream
of another door   sweet land of liberty   of thee of me   in the burning
beast where whoever stokes the fire and turns the knob
is righteous   is the liberty bell's hard shell   in the land of our fathers
our fathers our fathers   the clapper of the women's laced boots
the women's high heels   the women's bare feet   that do not sound like bells
from inside   that do not sound like singing   but the snorting
of ancient pipes to the tubes to the sky of I don't believe   and she was paid
and she wants   she only   she   sweet sweet land   sweet lamb
of a girl in the quiet that was never quiet in the prolonged burning
of the woods and the rills that is just a pretty word for a stream
where a girl should take her clothes off and the bull will come the bear
will come in his suit of a beast and will be a prince inside so the girl should
kneel to be pawed   to be eaten   to believe he is who he says he is
and she should love him when he takes his fur off   and her mortal
tongue should wake to sing as it melts   of the pilgrims' pride   that she's saved
for him in the templed hills of the dark bronze body that is not
her body closed and cast into a form around her where she cries and it bellows
Great God our king and our fathers' God to thee and thee and let
freedom ring through its nose   and its breath   and the piped-to-silence
steam of her voice   hot enough inside to break the rocks.

The Rough Beast Goes to Outer Space

Why don't we just put everybody in a space outfit or something like that?
No. Seriously, I mean—
         —Stephen Moore, Trump Economic Task Force Advisor, April 2020

and outer space looks a lot like America
from inside the helmet, the glass curving

the sky back inward like "The Star Spangled Banner"
playing backwards from cassettes in the Satanic Panic

when people feared daycares-fathers-teachers-
coaches-someone blood-ritualing their children.

That collective hysteria like a constellation
with no real lines connecting star to star

to oh-say-can-you, yet people kept drawing them,
pointing at the sky—

because something has to be to blame
for this earth's devily worms and split-open Barbie heads

and kids with their knees all bloodied
from falling or having to kiss the dark lord's private parts:

sanctum sanctorum of the mythic fears that say
trust no one, not scientists, not doctors, not whoever

says they care—any warning fact boomeranging back
like the waning moon of reason

thrown so hard it makes the Rough Beast dizzy.
Though he's breathing through a *kind of ventilator*

built right into his *space outfit*, its oxygen pack, thirteen layers,
and hard upper torso like a puffed-out exoskeleton or a blowfish

with pads instead of spines. And the $12 million price tag
still dangling like Minnie Pearl's hat in *Hee Haw*,

cornpone humor and capitalism included
in *all these kinds of suits they're building now.*

Which, the economist says, we all may need to buy
to have a functioning economy, to plug America back

into neon *OPEN*—its own private zero gravity,
which is not what this feels like:

these envelopes in pressurized envelopes
the Beast can hardly hear inside, though someone's singing

that our flag was still there, pointing toward the moon—
because something has to be the answer

to an Earth so full of bodies that airports are doubling
as morgues and doctors are trussed up

in trash bags as shoppers wave big padded hands
like that video where Armstrong and Aldrin try to flatten

the flag that keeps whipping back away
like a trick birthday candle, as if America's wish

might not come true after all. Or might keep coming true
like the fairytale where the weaver asks

for two heads and four hands to weave faster,
but all his speed doesn't save him from the village

that fears now he's a demon, which the Rough Beast understands:
he's listened to the stock market

played forward and the speeches declaring we're winning,
and sometimes the stars look all bendable

rushing at his head, and it's lonely in this suit,
and each day the air seems thinner.

Field Blocks

Sometimes there is so much sky, you can't see
out the window. The trees are snow again; the snow
is April rewinding its genetic code. The mice born
CRISPRed are young when they ought to be old. Ought-
to-be is a placebo for control. No one knows exactly
what belongs to us. The moon keeps falling
into poems—*lozenge of love*, etc.—a pinpoint to point
to when the earth gets unsustainable. The earth is
always unsustainable. The trees shake off their own
branches, or the wind does. The circuitry of living
keeps short circuiting. Shifty labyrinth, which like *rhythm*
is a word that refuses to be spelled right. I wait for
the rickrack red to un-underline it, tell me I've stumbled
into rightness. Stumbling-into-rightness is the best

I've come to hope for. A nerve block that hits the nerve
and quells it. The dentist says I have anastomosis. Crossed
wiring. My upper lip goes numb when the root refuses;
the drill strikes lightning to my earlobe. There is no
explaining me. Or a one-word explanation. Aren't we all
open-mouthed in this season? Upended? *Pincushioned*
the dentist calls me on the fourteenth shot. I could make
metaphors. Gun laws/racism/redistricting. I could not
draw the line of my own nerves until they stun me. I am
desperate for the wrong right point for the needle to
deaden. I want a way outside my own mixed messages.
Each negation contains its own action, says a poet
I could call a frenemy if I wanted the truth to criss-
cross with politeness. Inside unclenching, *clenching*

my jaw. Teeth are exploding in record numbers now,
my dentist says. *In my whole career, I've never seen anything
like it.* We are always arriving at probabilities, stats,
which are not unmoonlike—something to point to if
our hands feel useless. Our own hands often feel useless.

We're in one vast stress dream. For years in my sleep, gum
hardened in my mouth into taffy-superglue, bonded my
teeth together. I kept pulling out wads, shards. I'd never
get it all. It's common for teens to dream they're not in control
because they aren't. Each negation contains its own action:
undreaming, unhurting. Can you feel your chin? I cannot,
but then this jolt of ragged, singed-nerve raw. *Burn-
out* is a noun now, plus a verb. I am trying to open my
mouth. Wider. Wider. We are waiting for my face to

unfeel itself. The dentist shows me a video. He's not
racing his Porche because racing is illegal. He's just
driving radar-jammer fast until the desert sky flies by
like a sci-fi wormhole tunneling into itself. Men do this
(I learn now) for fun: unracing, erasing themselves
to a single point. Is it wrong to draw a line to comfort
from his dangerous certainty? He's holding the drill
again. *Proceed to the route, proceed to the route, proceed to,*
the voice in my phone says when I'm lost. It sounds
like increasing agitation. Of course I'm projecting.
If I knew how to proceed, wouldn't I be proceeding?
Would-that-I-could can be an excuse for so much
inaction. If a system is broken, drive bracing for cliffs?
Drive faster to somewhere? Drive slower? Drive back-

wards? I'm lucky I'm unlikely to be pulled over. I'm
unnerved by danger, and the world is dangerous. Proceed
to the. Proceed to. I call the voice *Little Lady* as a joke
about sexism. It's not usually funny: sexism. Clench.
Unclench my jaw. The journalist shows Powerpoints
of college-football rape headlines, pro-sports rape
headlines. *Sports Illustrated* waited to break the story
about assaults until after the swimsuit issue. *Ask yourself,*
she said, *why that would be.* There are bodies to move,
bodies to be moved. Balls in the air, so to speak. Lines

on the field. First down. Second down. I waited tables
for a year at a sports bar and never understood more
than *football*. Each negation contains its action: the men
kept playing on the field on the screen despite me,

like once an orthodontist stroked my hair and called me
beautiful as he talked about giving me nitrous. I bolted like
pain through a hot nerve. If you see the route in time,
you can proceed to the route. If aggression is hardwired,
it must have anastomosis—spreading out cattywampus,
cockeyed, skewed, etc. I can smell my nerves burning. But
now can't feel them. Didn't I want this? Still, I'm braced
for tripwires. When your mouth is on fire, it's hard to open
wide enough to call out *Wolf, Wolf!* As a girl, I wanted to be
the girl in the movie, or was in love with the girl in the movie,
The Journey of Natty Gann. She's run away to find her father
at a place called *logging camp*. It's the Great Depression,
meaning economic, and other things. She's androgynous,
scrappy, and would-be-raped except the wolf she's adopted

(Wolf!) protects her. We're lucky if our daemons find us, if
we climb the right boxcars. If the tracks go where we think
they will. The tracks often go where we think they will when
we wish they wouldn't. It's easy to predict the punchlines.
After *Game of Thrones*, everyone wanted a wolf. Now shelters
are full of huskies. Dreaming wilderness is not the same as
having to clean its paws. Burnout is a noun, a verb, a land-
scape. We're wandering through it. Scientists are making real
synthetic dolphins. They're indistinguishable in the Sea World
show. Look at the moon on their un-skin. Isn't it beautiful?
Most answers go with too many questions. We're in the age of
the humane if you ignore the inhumanity, the wild-branching
monstrousness. Soon, someone will engineer teeth with no
nerves, so I can't be miswired. I'll open my perfect mouth.

America: Hepatomancy

If the liver is the source of blood: if the liver is the source
of life: if the people live with blood, visceral, on the sidewalks; the news
ticker divining *Police Kill:* the news ticker divining *Supporters Shout;*

if the people mow the bright green golf-course grass
of battlefields: Pea Ridge, Antietam: dust the sky with flags
and mow the grass, and the liver blinks toxic as a neon sign,

and the men move the pegs in the stock market
and the men water the grass; and *Hate* and *Hate;* and the men
say *Let the President;* and the people say *Compassion;* and the liver

reveals its dark deities on the walls of buildings;
its ancient symbols; and the liver reveals the people's bodies
coursing strange bloods; and the men lean in closer to observe

how their pockets fill; and the liver shines like the knife
that opens it; the liver shines like a safe word on a tongue;
and someone says, *It's all consensual.* And someone says, *Help.*

The Rough Beast Takes a Painting Class

The surface of American society is covered with a layer of democratic paint,
but from time to time one can see the old aristocratic colours breaking through.
      —Alexis de Tocqueville, Democracy in America

The teacher says white is not truly a color,
containing as it does, all wavelengths of visible light.

She says the Rough Beast's claws might be useful later
for scraffito—to scratch back through to what's beneath:

cyan and *magenta; Goldman-Sachs* and *Donald Trump.*
The teacher says *Trump is not a color.* But everyone knows

he's on the wheel between *Versailles-mirror-hall* and *rosebush*
with limp orange petals and a shitstorm of thorns. All the brushes' bristles

are made of his hair. It's hard to keep the paint from clumping.
The Best Color Wheel is segregated into swaths—no way to spin it

like a Twister spinner: *blueviolettangerinecharcoalforesttealyellow.*
No way to step on two colors with the same foot at once.

The teacher says there is no color called *Keep Out,*
although the Beast has seen it. In pointillism, the world

sieves into so many tiny dots—a thousand points of light—
until it's hard to tell which dot amid the swan boat   dot

parasol   dot   lakes with a golfcourse   dot   is democracy.
She shows battleships dazzle-painted in Cubist camouflage:

black and white angles and stripes like a flotilla of zebras.
This was supposed to confuse torpedoes. She doesn't say

if the lesson shows the limits of deception or imagination.
She arranges a still life to keep everything still: a peacock's

hues simmered down to two glimmering feathers, a skull
resting loudly by a fruitbowl. *No one would eat a Cezanne apple,*

she explains, meaning people want realism more than truth.
Good apples do not complain about the light that hits them.

The Years I Lived Beneath the Lake

I wandered antique malls where the light was so dry
you would not have known
I was drowning, and the gloves were small
and tight and stitched with monograms of strangers,
and the real-iron irons stuck their stiff
black noses in the air beside my ankles like dogs
and I could say, *good iron, good iron,*
heel as I moved among them, twenty and married
and lonely in a way that only objects understood:
handkerchiefs and tatted doilies and neon
tubes blaring, like trumpets in the ocean, *OPEN*,
though it was impossible
to know what the *OPENESS* belonged to
except itself or a solid wall or the doll's
eyes staring sun-burst-
crazed at dust motes.
What did I want? Stillness and a handwritten price,
though I never bought anything;
poor and scared of my life
rubbing off on them: these objects that existed
perfectly without me: the brown swan ashtray floating
in its own dark glaze; the cherry-poxed bread box;
the pedestaled glass cake plate's
caustic of green light beneath itself: one inedible
wedge of hunger
that would fade when the lights switched off,
then return again. The mannequins blinking,
necklaces slung around their narrow necks
harmlessly. Here there were no backstories at all.
The clean-cracked, glue-ridged pitcher
with its discount sticker: numbered
by some dull Midwestern God who'd laid aside the chaff
from other chaff: each assigned its proper, jumbled
stall. I'd come days I was depressed, he was
depressed, we were fighting, he had hit me, my body

on the couch with its stiff brown pillows that had been
there when we moved in, that were ours now
somehow. Here: ruffle-edged lampshades and wash-
boards and gloves scorched at the tips by fire
or what was maybe only dirt. No one had driven through
this traffic light propped on its side, unlit, maybe
unlightable. No one living wore such pleated skirts.

Mean High Water

an American gyre

The sign says *Mean High Water* where the trail reaches / the sudden boat-bob-struck-salt sparkle of the estuary / meaning I am too late or too early to cross here / meaning only the water's average height / but what does average mean or matter if I'll only ever be here once in my muddy shoes / the sea deep-unwalkable / shoulder-high, higher / halyards knocking out there / a tide can do this, has / darted the earth with light-needle, light-silver ripples / caustics, they're called like a sense of humor backed by a mean high laugh-track in childhood / when it still seemed enough humor, enough guts of some kind could eat through the rust clotting the world's wrong bolts together / the way your mother told you Coca Cola did in a mechanic's bucket / so you still can't drink it / dark fizz of legend and warning at the edge of everything. / What you really need's a tide chart, / some parts of this world predictable. / Even a waterfall can be met with a barrel if you know in time / to take cardboard and string to the cooper / cut and tied into a prototype / because ingenuity and bootstrap-up-pulling is how it's done / in America where *charm's in limited supply and refusing to stretch* / though that's someone else's life again / poising on the brink *for a moment, and then—* / You could swim maybe if you had to / sodden pack on your back / but the trail detours: fields, ditches / ocean just a metaphor your map insists on / *keep the coast on your left* / keep walking / keep keeping up / because it's up to you, buddy, lady, lucky duck to sew your heart-shaped pillow for Niagara. / Your first falls as a child on the Maid of the Mist / that pounding dazzling above you / like show-stoppers in musicals your parents loved / the river ripping off its plain grey dress to reveal sequins, / belting out *I've always been thunderous* / the way you dreamed your dusty nothing-special-of-a-life with the brush-snakey creek on the old Teague land / the semi your uncle drove, his trailer, the dog that scared you / someday would whirl up into a life that glistened. / *Mean High Water* that you can't help thinking is the perfect band name / for music inside you've never dared play: not tidy, but tidal / country and punk and neither exactly /

strings gleaming so bright they might cut your fingers if you tried to touch them / like that upright bass the bassist played shoeless through Idaho winters / crisp concert black above bare splayed toes. / Even before you knew, didn't you know? / It's where the music came from: up from their bones. / Not quirkiness but any shoes he could afford would hurt. / Poverty too smashed toes of your paternal grandfather and nine one-room siblings. / Two generations back, but what do generations mean or matter? / Your little toes born curled inward (inbred?) so you step on them stepping / blisters pulsing over whorled calluses / though some poor mean pride says hike on anyway / what doesn't kill you makes you something / *It came to me in a flash of light,* Annie Edson Taylor said after / first woman / person / to pose for pictures after (live through) plummeting Niagara's eighteen stories / 3,000 tons of water per second / because she saw no choice / out-of-work charm-school teacher in 1901 / single 63-year-old woman at the ledge of another hard, turning century / this same brutal country. / Sewed pillows—oblong and heart-shaped— / took a prototype of cardboard and string to a beer-barrel cooper / paid to have herself rowed into the gyring. / *At the brink, the barrel did what I predicted it would do, paused for a moment / then made the awful plunge. / I hoped,* she said, *to aid myself financially.* / Pull yourself down up over the bootstrappy falls! / Sink or swim, dearies. / Sink or swim or plunge! / Lucky future girl, you climbed into barrels called scholarships, neat-hammered boards of high S.A.T. scores. / Then marriage: waterlogged, fist-slogged. / Love's mean high water all you'd ever known to want. / Sinead O'Connor's *If you said jump in a river I would because it would probably be a good idea.* / Tenuous brink of *probably*— / that lure of maybe not, maybe hurt, maybe hitting the rocks is what living is. / Who told you different? / Not your parents / or that boy, man, teenage sweetheart raised in a trailer with sometimes power. / Unpredictable / unhinged / not (you shouted to yourself) unloveable / even when he hit you like rapids churning against skin. / Here's where the barrel leaks. / Where Leonard Cohen says the light gets in. / (Build a better barrel.) / (A stronger ribcage.) / Stand in the mist of the Bass Pro Shop waterfall: electric-pumped into the fake rock pool built for testing fishing rods /

the closest at nineteen (married lonely) to Iguazu, Victoria, Angel as you'd get. / Taxidermied monkeys clutching boxes of Cracker Jacks on branches above. / Midwestern pretty light on the fiberglass boats. / Buy a better one to row upstream / Put it on layaway / Pay and pay. / *Freedom's just another word for nothing left to lose* / your favorite line in your favorite song that you believed was romantic then. / How did *I* become *you* for so long anyway? / (What a perfect barrel, big enough for anyone.) / Never mind the head-spinning. / How well I folded myself into school seats, marriages, too-tight skirts, my passport, the dammed-up lakeshores, / divorce. / Divorced. / Stepping out dizzy. / *Good god she's alive!* / Blaring of boat horns. / Though that's someone else's life again— / Build a better prototype for womanhood. / Cardboard / String / By *prototype,* what do we even mean? / Aren't our lives proof-of-concept? / *I would rather face a cannon,* she said, *than ever again.* / Posing with her barrel like a racehorse / til "unscrupulous promoters" / stole it / left her broke / broken. / *Goddess of the Water,* papers called her / as if she controlled the falling or the falls. / *The risks are all the stuff around you.* / *You just have to hope that you get pushed up,* / a master swimmer said. / Fold the body into curtsies. / Fold the body in and in and / *If not rocks, the turbulence, the darkness, the cold, bruising current.* / *Charm's in limited supply and refusing to stretch* / that song I played on repeat as my mother died / She'd hemorrhaged / from my first breaths / code blue. / Her body a waterfall of grief and skin and / too easy to say that's the reason I've never felt safe here / anywhere / Row me to the center / no, I'm scared / row me back again. / Water finds its own level. / That's what I'm afraid of / teenage foster brother boyfriend / made me take my clothes off / not made / here's a waterfall you should jump into / this river probably / I wanted to / my mother loved him / thought he was a good song for me to sing my life away to / pretty dammed water of my body bruising. / Uncle driving drunk again / uncle with a shotgun / cousin blacking out from truck fumes. / I used to say white trash (if I admitted it) / *white* I've learned now racist / as if most *trash* isn't / my family was / is / all on the same land of those too-small shoes. / Low on daredevilry. / High on gas fumes. / Pull yourself up by your bootstraps meaning, originally, *try to do the impossible.* / Sort of a joke at first. / *Probably,* one reporter says, *that says something about America.* / Detour farther. / Hope to find the coast again. / The Pacific Trash Vortex out there somewhere / turning turning widening / like Raging Rivers at amusement parks my family loved / climb into your padded boat for the rocks that aren't / while the real rocks / let's not talk about them. / Sister taken for $9000 / all her savings / by a man who said he poured foundations / She wouldn't want me saying this. / *Freedom's just another name for* / Build a barrel marked language around anxiety / Build a barrel marked silence. / *There's no wind in this part of your voyage.* / *I repeat:* / *we are gyrating motionless.* / *There's no—* / What would it sound like? The bottom of the waterfall of self? / Always something between the music of ourselves and us. / Splash of the rocks / thrash of all those bass notes / rushing / of my own strange familiar blood. / Swim in the water I'm given. / Lucky American girl / depressive / and living. / Spectators on shore shouting *stop drowning, start waving* or / *I'm happy, I hope you're happy too* / like Bowie striding in that video down a beach / oversaturated sexy psychedelia of 80s childhood / Mean High Water a band he could have fronted / known how to wade in. / Though didn't he also prey on teens then? / *I remember him looking like God and having me over a table* / one says not regretting it. / No way across but around and around / the swirling inland of here. / Like a lifeguard I knew / used to swim a Florida lake / full of alligators / each night at sunset / claiming it was the quickest way / to prove what a man he was / he was / tried later for scamming seniors / fake pharmaceuticals. / Fake jungle vines but the monkeys are real / looking down on America. / Which way is the trail marked *I agreed to any of it?* / When did anyone? / Like the white poet, of the old Black man he thought had liked his company: / *I learned, later, that he was simply terrified,* / *And that a gang of boys had crept up, earlier, with sticks.* / Barrel of civility / barrel of a smile / Barrel of words around everything / *For the earth will be filled with the knowledge of the Lord as the waters cover the sea,* as the sign just told me. / How did God first get here through a sort-of rape scene? / And how do waters lay on sea / like a girl over a table? / *We are gyrating motionless* / And the water that covers the sea / which one is shining? / We don't teach those questions here. /

What's beneath the water? / Sea. / But what's the sea made of? / Trash maybe / sinking time / women in lace-up boots pillowed by their own *ambitiondesperationfear* / when inside our crooked toes are swollen pruning swelling like wet wood / how will we walk from here? / Anywhere, / water finds its own level. / Freedom's just another name for / uncle with a shotgun. / That's what I'm afraid of: / thrash of all those bass notes. / Let's not talk about them. / What doesn't kill you makes you something / unpredictable. / Belting out *I've always been thunderous,* / *depressive* / (if not rocks, the turbulence, the darkness, the cold, bruising current). / Pull yourself up by your bootstraps meaning, originally, *try to do the impossible*: / that song I played on repeat as my mother died, / poising on the brink *for a moment, and then*— / Fold the body in and in and. / Hope to find the coast again, / like Bowie striding in that video down a beach / darted the earth with light-needle, light-silver ripples / made me take my clothes off. / (Some parts of this world predictable.) / Here's a waterfall you should jump into! / Or that boy, man, teenage sweetheart raised in a trailer with sometimes power. / Country and punk and neither exactly. / Broken / (even before you knew, didn't you know?) / I used to say white trash (if I admitted it) / like Raging Rivers at amusement parks my family loved. / Taxidermied monkeys clutching boxes of Cracker Jacks on branches above. / Sink or swim or plunge! / Sort of a joke at first / (as if most trash isn't). / The closest at nineteen (married lonely) to Iguazu, Victoria, Angel as you'd get: / stepping out dizzy, / sodden pack on your back / when it still seemed enough humor, enough guts of some kind could eat through the rust clotting the world's wrong bolts together: / cousin blacking out from truck fumes, / the semi your uncle drove, his trailer, the dog that scared you / rushing, / then made the awful plunge. / But the trail detours: fields, ditches, / your little toes born curled inward (inbred?) so you step on them stepping, / pay and pay. / My family was / white. I've learned now racist. / Like the white poet, of the old Black man he thought had liked his company: / *I'm happy, I hope you're happy too.* / This same brutal country / high on gas fumes, / blaring of boat horns. / Uncle driving drunk again / to prove what a man he was. / Cut and tied into a prototype. / Each night at sunset /

never mind the head-spinning. / *Freedom's just another word for nothing left to lose.* / I wanted to / divorce / poverty. Too-smashed toes of your paternal grandfather and nine one-room siblings / all on that same land of the too-small shoes. / (It's where the music came from: up from their bones.) / *You just have to hope that you get pushed up.* / When did anyone? / Tenuous brink of *probably*— / keep walking / the sea deep-unwalkable, / meaning only the water's average height. / Swim in the water I'm given: / oversaturated sexy psychedelia of 80s childhood. / (*Probably,* one reporter says, *that says something about America.*) / Dark fizz of warning and legend at the edge of everything. / *It came to me in a flash of light,* Annie Edson Taylor said after / *mean high water.* That you can't help thinking is the perfect band name—/ *Goddess of the Water*— papers called her / like showstoppers in musicals your parents loved. / Charm's in limited supply and refusing to stretch / two generations back, but what do generations mean or matter? / We don't teach those questions here. / Lucky American girl / (out-of-work charm-school teacher in 1901), / her body, a waterfall of grief and skin and / fold-the-body-into-curtsies. / *There's no wind in this part of your voyage.* / Sinking time / all her savings / paid to have herself rowed into the gyring. / Barrel of a smile / full of alligators. / (We are gyrating motionless.) / That lure of maybe not, maybe hurt, maybe hitting the rocks is what living is: / (*this river probably / thought he was a good song for me to sing my life away to.* / *No. I'm scared.* / *What's beneath the water?* / *Splash of the rocks.* / *Pretty damned water of my body bruising.* / *Which way is the trail marked I agreed to any of it?* / *Row me back again,* / *low on daredevilry.* / *Build a better barrel* / *not made* / *in America where charm's in limited supply and refusing to stretch* / (We are gyrating motionless.) / Spectators on shore shouting *stop drowning, start waving* or / *No way across but around and around!* / 3,000 tons of water per second / turning turning widening / unhinged. / Code blue / strings gleaming so bright they might cut your fingers if you tried to touch them— / *Here's where the barrel leaks* / *women in lace-up boots pillowed by their own ambitiondesperationfear* / *meaning I am too late or too early to cross here* / *while the real rocks* / *build a barrel marked silence.* / (She wouldn't want me saying this.) / *I would rather face a cannon,* she said, *than ever again* / *to take cardboard and string to the cooper / I repeat.* / What would it sound like? The bottom of the waterfall of self? / The river ripping off its plain grey dress to reveal sequins / of my own strange familiar blood. / The swirling inland of here- / stand-in-the-mist of the Bass Pro Shop waterfall: electric-pumped into the fake rock pool built for testing fishing rods. / That pounding dazzling above you, / not (you shouted to yourself) unloveable. / Barrel of words around everything. / How well I folded myself into school seats, marriages, too-tight skirts, my passport, the dammed-up lakeshores. / Used to swim a Florida lake claiming it was the quickest way / (halyards knocking out there) / and that a gang of boys had crept up, earlier, with sticks / known how to wade in, / like a lifeguard I knew / (though didn't he also prey on teens then?) / The risks are all the stuff around you / and the water that covers the sea: / shoulder-high, higher: / the Pacific Trash Vortex out there somewhere: / string / cardboard / fake pharmaceuticals / fake jungle vines but the monkeys are real- / midwestern. Pretty light on the fiberglass boats. / Caustics, they're called like a sense of humor backed by a mean high laugh-track. In childhood, / trash maybe / someday would whirl up into a life that glistened / the way your mother told you Coca Cola did in a mechanic's bucket. / Where Leonard Cohen says the light gets in. / My mother loved him. / Mean High Water a band he could have fronted, / crisp concert black above bare splayed toes, / til unscrupulous promoters— / tried later for scamming seniors— / stole it / because it's up to you, buddy, lady, lucky duck to sew your heart-shaped pillow for Niagara! / Pull yourself down up over the bootstrappy falls! / Single 63-year-old woman at the ledge of another hard, turning century, / sister taken for $9000 / because she saw no choice. / *I hoped*, she said, *to aid myself financially.* / Though that's someone else's life-again- / left-her-broke. / Aren't our lives proof of concept: / what you really need's a tide chart? / Though some poor mean pride says hike on anyway. / Keep keeping up, / climb into your padded boat for the rocks that aren't / ocean, just a metaphor. Your map insists on / build a barrel marked language around anxiety: / *And how do waters lay on sea? / How will we walk from here? / But what's the sea made of? / But what does average mean or matter if I'll only ever be here once in my muddy shoes* / blisters *pulsing over whorled calluses?* / The sign says *Mean High Water* where the trail reaches: / even when he hit you like rapids churning against skin, / he was / your favorite line in your favorite song that you believed was romantic then. / Love's mean high water all you'd ever known to want / so you still can't drink it. / Lucky future girl, you climbed into barrels called scholarships. Neat-hammered boards of high S.A.T., scores / for music inside you've never dared play: not tidy, but tidal; / not your parents'. / I remember him looking like God and having me over a table / to pose for pictures after live-through plummeting Niagara's eighteen stories— / Your first falls as a child on the Maid of the Mist. / *At the brink, the barrel did what I predicted it would do, paused for a moment*— / Then marriage: waterlogged, fist-slogged / divorced / (one says not regretting it) / by a man who said he poured foundations / I learned, later, that he was simply terrified, / teenage. Foster-brother-boyfriend. / Not quirkiness but any shoes he could afford would hurt. / Too easy to say that's the reason I've never felt safe here, / like a girl over a table. / Who told you different? / Sinead O'Connor's *If you said jump in a river I would because it would probably be a good idea.* / Even a waterfall can be met with a barrel if you know in time. / As if she controlled the falling or the falls, / took a prototype of cardboard and string to a beer-barrel cooper. / (What a perfect barrel, big enough for anyone, / when inside our crooked toes are swollen pruning swelling like wet wood.) / By prototype what do we even mean? / Buy a better one to row upstream. / Sink or swim, dearies! / *You could swim maybe if you had to,* / a master swimmer said. / Keep the coast on your left. / *For the earth will be filled with the knowledge of the Lord as the waters cover the sea,* as the sign just told me. / How did God first get here through a sort-of rape scene? / First woman / *good god, she's a live / person!* / sewed pillows: oblong and heart-shaped. / She'd hemorrhaged / a stronger ribcage / because ingenuity and bootstrap-up-pulling is how it's done. / Always something between the music of ourselves and us, / like that upright bass the bassist played shoeless through Idaho winters, / posing with her barrel like a racehorse. / Barrel of civility / and living. / Though that's someone else's life again, / looking down on America, / the way you dreamed your dusty nothing-special-of-a-life with the

brush-snakey creek on the old Teague land / is / sea: / the sudden
boat-bob struck-salt sparkle of the estuary. / From my first breaths /
a tide can do this, has. / How did *I* become *you* for so long anyway? /
Which one is shining? / Build a better prototype for womanhood. /
Put it on layaway. / Row me to the center. / There's no / detour farther.

The Rough Beast Would Like The Future To Be Clear

That he is made of the past like a junk shop
with split-frame washboards
and dolls with crazed, crazy eyes: some composite
that doesn't age well. Like human history. Some experimental glue
and plastic and silicon carbide known to be
flammable and cause cancer
in the state of California (how dangerous everything is
if we read the little tags). That he is tagless
and lethal as any living thing. Made
of single-use bicycle tires and animal cookies
with ice-rinky icing and nose bleeds
from the first few weeks of antidepressants, a dark joke
turned inside out. A bad surprise party. That he is made
like all of us of darkness and inopportune floodlights, of falling
from frying pans to fires and back.
That he is our brain that is an egg that is
sizzling in that 1980s anti-drug ad
that forgot how few people eat raw eggs
and how much we want to escape ourselves. He is our brain
that's like that Simon game with its flashing
lights in patterns repeating repeating: red blue green
blue blue red, like a random emergency.
That he is us trying to get the pattern right.
That he's a myth to tell us why we never do, why we lose
every person, our sanity, much
kindness. Why every generation someone shouts, *My mind's
not right*, and people nod and sing along, stuck between future
and finity: a word we use less often than its opposite
because we live in it. Its one-way-exit box.
That he is made of it too: whatever we've ever been made of. Electric
kettles on the fritz, color-coded file
drawers and brain scans and a thousand
lost pencils. The distance between where we're going
and always are: flashing pop-up ads, horoscopes, horror,
red wheelbarrows repurposed as junk-store planters

because so much depends on
feeling as if something depends on us. That he is
inside whatever fur we imagine him, an inside
joke like all of us. *I guess you had to be there.* That we say this
when we can't remember what was funny either. That he's less
mythology, more mothball, like the Goodwill sweater
we try on saying *Someone made this for me,*
though we know whoever made it
never knew there was an us at all.

Lake Chacolet

August, 2021

My father wants me to stop calling it *the apocalypse,* the air all moneyed the color of pennies in a dirty fountain, both of us trying to catch our breath. If this were a nightmare, coarse-grained sandpaper would have gritted out the clouds, the sky, the lake. This is August in the inland West. Smoke meshes everything like a window screen inside a window screen inside dirty glass. My swimming arms, my father in a kayak he's learning to paddle, turning like a man in a slow-motion whirlpool. The fires are states away, invisible. The AQI scorches up: red to purple to maroon like a ladder to the center of the sun. The dogs on shore are going ape-shit for floating sticks. Call it oxygen deprivation: my fear they'll swim out in the lake and bite me. My father says, *You're too far away.* But who can tell distance now? Aren't I bleary-eyed, bobbing like a chew toy? The lakefloor mud is toxic with heavy metals, waiting to rise with one bad algae bloom. It's common knowledge. It's *Wash Your Pets and Feet* signs. To call the lake the *Superfund* it is would make the waterfront property less valuable. If *blue is big enough for a Dutch man's britches,* I learned as a child, rain will blow over. There's not a speck of rain nor blue to see. Call it oxygen deprivation: the puffy clouds I'm missing: not a memory of sky but those 1990s cotton-t-shirt sheets, a summer-camp fantasy of sleep rolled in its own little tote bag. *Remember carrying the sky in your arms? Sleeping peacefully?* I don't say because my father never went to camp, grew up in foster care in the 1950s, fearing TV people trapped inside an iron lung: white metal tube of isolation like a nowhere spaceship. He'd say we're lucky to be here at all. Is saying it. *The apocalypse is Revelations mumbo-jumbo; just because things are changing doesn't mean it's the end.* Everywhere, orange-grey ash-light unhorizons us. Is there some saying like *If the future is big enough for?* The dogs are barking; their people are standing on a new treated dock that most days ends in pretty water. I'm swimming through mine tailings, or will be once the chemistry tilts just so. A whole lake can backflip. A sky can vanish, has vanished. *It's just shorthand,* I try to tell him, dog-paddling, eyes-stinging. But he's already facing away again. He keeps turning circles because he's never rowed a kayak. He wants to stay close beside me because he was an abandoned child; because he loves me. He's not denying science. He's row row rowing like that song he used to sing me, this scenic Superfund site on fire, in a little inflatable boat.

Closed Captions

One week in, the captions on our laptop movie keep announcing, *ominous music intensifying* as the branches creak, *ominous music intensifying* as the family's goat, Black Phillip, turns out to be the devil. We have all closed our doors around whatever we live with. Greenland and South Africa have banned liquor for health, or to try to staunch the beatings. We have all sanitized our doorknobs and closed our doors, although the news saws open holes for a pipe-organ Wurlitzering ominousness as we grind our coffee, as Perfume Genius intones *'Cause it's singing through your body And I'm carried by the sound.* In the movie, which is balanced on my husband's knees in bed, the children circle the goat, obliviously singing to it, as we once held other children's hands, chanting *Ring around the rosie,* falling dizzily to lawns. In each generation, someone spills the secret: *that song's about the plague,* and children shiver, hearing, inside their music-box play, something ominous and ancient. Someone has turned up the soundtrack of that ancient world. In the movie, which is called *The Witch,* an actual witch is snatching and grinding up children. This is what the Puritan family fears, exiled at the edge of the forest, and they are right to fear it. Obviousness goes so far it circles back to the unlikely. It is terrifying when what we fear is flying through the air really is flying. We are alone, or we are not alone. When our neighbors set off fireworks, concussive, staggered barely by air, it sounds so much like shots, I think first *double homicide, suicide.* We've all closed in whoever we live with. We've all closed down around our own anxieties. I am mildly afraid of the water glass I touch after touching the mail. Mildly surprised the person in the white horror-movie mask is not a pranking friend but a Zoom bomber who listens in, tugging at a rubber chin, as my friends in Italy tell about barricades, death tolls. There are the wrong kinds of masks, or no masks. In the movie, the oldest daughter keeps insisting the evil isn't her, but her parents are so afraid they trust no one. It is part of horror that sometimes everyone dies. Part of American religiosity to believe in exceptional salvation and sin. There are politicians grinding up facts and profit and time. We should have seen this coming, or we did. We have closed the entire internet into our houses, so when that masked face stares, I think, *What if he hurts us?* But none of us is really *here* to hurt. I am reading facts. I am trying to stay rational. My friends and I lean toward each other's small, boxed faces. It's hard to hear the words in real time, though sometimes they catch us, jolting, seconds after, to our open mouths. My husband and I can't understand all the seventeenth-century Puritan brogue, so we've turned on these captions, but no one is speaking now. We are at the edge of the wilderness, a place maybe we've always been. We're spinning between fear and safety and fear and. The branches are creaking. There's *ominous music intensifying,* though it just did seconds ago. It is part of horror that what could be the end isn't. Sometimes it's also part of being lucky. Is the music actually louder than last time? Or does the caption mean louder than the goat and voices? Or that even simple acts, like breathing, like sitting in this bed, are intensifying?

The Goth Comes Clean About Decay

Man, like all animals, is glass and can return to glass.
    —*Johann Becher,* Physica Subterranea, *1669*

Given the choice, I would also rather be a vase
than a cadaver—*hideous, disgusting,* Becher calls the dead
with their skin squelch, their ears packed up with dirt
like crusty flower pots. Lucky the *ponderable parts of flame*
can pass through our pores and make us what we are
already—silica-slick, yearning toward transparence—
window glass with snug velvet curtains sashed to let
light through: our ancestors arranged as ball jars
cradling water, hyacinth, lilies in symmetrical bowls
tinted, by the nature of man, *with a hint of narcissus—*

    Once, my husband and I watched his tall goth student
    and her friends descend toward the water at Miami Beach
    at twilight—the too-perfect, sun-starkened sand cooling
    at last to cratered shadow, and them, vapor-light pale,
    black jeans on even as they swam. *The plight of the goth
    in the tropics,* we joked, though we too felt most akin
    to the South's slumping porches, veils of Spanish moss
    like griefs carried into the trees by the same old weather
    that'd topple Art Deco shopping malls and tucked-butt
    rollerbladers in spandex skins. None of us immune then.

My mother's friend, skin crystalled by scleroderma,
could hold a pencil in her clawed hand if a helper
put it there, write, but not, herself, unhold it. She'd
sit in a wheelchair at her desk, stalking crabbed calligraphic
letters on thin pages, her skin daily shrinking closer
on its way to smothering her lungs, heart, stomach;
her jaw welding against tongue, that pencil nubbed
into the hole between thumb, forefinger. She'd paint

too with brush stuck in: flowers that drooped as she
must have wished to, spilling the rigid vase.

      Like frogs' dill green leaching into a hot-glass soup,
      Becher said each creature will lend its shade, distinct,
      and subtle—our dead bodies clouding milk-white or
      yellow as daffodils. No gag of nose bones collapsing
      under dirt, no blub of body, just sweet, rootless petals
      blushing and swelling open like the air exhaled down
      pipe to molten silica—human breath at last made
      permanent. What else could glass be, then, but alchemy?
      What else could a body be? Not quite metal, not rock,
      not returnable to what it was before it hardened.

It's a simple sine wave from ghost to glass—away
from gristle. Ash heap of mother at root-rot tree;
grandmother thrown at ocean that sloshed her back,
muck-puddling in tidepools. At least fire scorches,
crizzles, shatters, before earth's slow mulch. *Chemists
are a strange class of mortal,* Becher wrote, *to seek pleasure
among smoke and vapor, soot and flame*—yet who instead
pleasures at the world's drains? Dredged hairball and
pus; decay's transformations? Better believe the body
phlogiston: holding inside all the force it needs for flame.

      Melodrama, one writer says, is what happens to people
      you don't know: meaning *make your characters whole.*
      Did I not know—those years I dreamed Wuthering
      winds in the Ozark hills—myself and my own bored
      fears of flesh: simple and pimpled and hairbrushed?
      In one dream, I'd been locked in the Crescent Hotel:
      ghosts waltzing the rug's Byzantium, stripped gears
      in the music box of time. Drama, friends, is boring.
      I wanted *melo*—song of phones from unrented rooms,
      a friend's mom, at the switchboard, swore rang.

As a teenager, I craved air verging on combustible.
I wore black in summer—feared polka-dot cheerful
freckles on my nose, pastel silk flowers, everything
kitschy with solace. Give me Lear's hand that smelled
of mortality; eyes in old photos: ancestors in naïve,
tragic poses of thinking they're still alive. Give me
lion-claw bathtubs curved like rowboats—Charon
scouring bodies back to absence. I *pitied the bathtub
its forced embrace of the human form,* believed in death
like a song I hummed as my own life kept flowing.

    Too easy to say I've gotten older; mortality's
    not fun. I wear yellow for cheer in winter—fear
    hairs re-coiling counters, drains' throating mold.
    At Kutna Hora's ossuary, the skulls strung up as
    chandeliers feel gratuitous. I worry at swallowing—
    the insistent hurt; my throat's pink, I imagine, dark-
    pebbled with cancer. Dirt sticks to the flesh, magnet
    to metal grit, or felt boards for Bible Study: grubby
    animals, floppy ark, too-soft dove. Southern child,
    shouldn't I have known this? The flood full of mud.

My ex-husband watched his brother die of AIDS,
sputtering blood beside a cage of finches. Years after,
he wanted to start a business of funeral urns, throwing clay
with bent sides, dark glazes. I use one for compost still—
a small goth joke, though don't touch the muck-slither
innards. I knew his brother only as blood splotched
on a pillow my husband slept on nightly. Guilty survivor,
given the choice, he would have carried the vase of his
brother everywhere, just to feel the fear again before
breakage. Given the choice, I say, as if there is one.

When, Like Garden Spiders from Space Orbit, We Return

Two garden spiders named Arabella and Anita were used to study how orbiting earth would impact spiders' ability to spin webs. Arabella spun a fairly symmetric web even though the thread thickness varied—something that earthbound spiders don't experience.
    —Elizabeth Dohrer, "Laika the Dog & the First Animals in Space"

We will weave a web the size of the rose bush
all over the rose bush the way people throw their arms around
relatives in airports, as if they are trying to attach
a thousand thin silk threads—of love plus gravity plus where-have-you-
been-so-long?—to their feet and shuffly suitcases and knit-capped heads; we will
spin knit caps with tassels for everyone out of space dust and our own
exhausted bodies; we will not talk about what it felt like to spin up there
when we were also spinning. We will not say *eight eyes full of darkness,* or *that long
unanchored pulling,* like trying to unwrap moonlight from its tightwrapped
spool of moon, so it's no wonder it wavered from us like arcane geometry—thinning
and thickening like we were seeing it from dimensions different than we'd ever thought of.
We will say *cucumber leaf! pumpkin with its unwinding, tethered coils;* we will launch
from them, dirtily, earthily. We will not ask what the point was. We will
return like a radio transmission out of the desert, when the song
reattaches its filaments of breathy voice to music, and the rasping of the wind
is over; the rasping of space blanking past us. We will crawl
back to what we love, as if it is earth-mist ordinary, as if we are not dizzy
still, lank-legged. We will offer what we have always offered:
out of everything, most days, fairly symmetric. We will look
down down into the leafy wet of spring, or whatever this new season is.

Eclipses

for Dylan

After you lose your wedding ring, everything turns
into circles: silver rivets puckering
our bedframe; a quarter clanging in the dryer; bottlecaps; keyring
in a shirt pocket; one bolt against the car's
Kettle-chip-crushed carpet. Your fingers digging into grit, trying
to match the perfect holes of *where, when*—like finding the sky's
one blue through a cyanometer: a circle for the air, a ring of shades:
light to darker (but the clouds keep moving; the sky is dimming,
brightening unpredictably). You are kneeling at the parking meter
grass; I am kneeling with a flashlight. Silver rivets. Filthy carpet,
dimes beneath the driver's seat. It is less gone
if we are always looking. One week ago, everyone stared
at the familiar sky through NASA glasses. The radio warned:
You can go blind in just an instant. White crescent shadows climbed
every tree trunk. We thought we knew where the sky
was. Sometimes it hurts to love anything this fiercely.
The moon is just an object. The sun is just an object
behind an object. A shoebox can turn the sky inside out.
I have looked in one. I do not understand it really. Time
has one perfect hole for the day we stood on a rocky beach
vowing *forever*. Rocks under my heels, your ox-blood boots,
our fingers. You have dug through banana peels, egg shells,
coffee filters crushed like midden; you are checking inside
the yellow plastic gloves you've worn, like you could have
lost it inside their fingers while you were looking. We are vowing
with each thought. Drain. Soap. Olive oil at the Co-op.
Bottle neck. Zipper. Pocket seam. Wad of paper. We mean
love love love love, I think, but we're too close to see it. Once
I saw a ring of feathers in a county museum in the Ozarks: *Angel's
Crown or Death Crown* said the index card typed up beside it.
*A sign from God that forms inside your feather pillow when you
go up to heaven. Or a sign of the witchcraft that has killed you.*

I didn't expect to feel afraid when the sun started leaving.
What has existed still exists somewhere, says some theory;
any symbol is just a symbol. I am circling words in the dictionary
in my mind: places, places, places. You have turned
the mattress on its edge to shake out sheets we have washed
and shaken. I have never seen the feathers
in my own pillow. Some things should not be stared
into directly. Knife drawer, cat food, q-tip box, plastic produce bags. It is all
we can talk about. Memory is irresponsible. One day we'll wake
oblivious again to the rivets that hold this bed together. We'll drop
potato chips by accident beneath the bucket seats on road trips, wrinkled
shadows of golden fields spreading out below us. Your hands
on the steering wheel as we make fun of our own jokes
then circle back to laughing. What else
did I ever mean? I should reach across
to hold your hand, just my fingers against your fingers.

The Rough Beast Talks to the Falcon

if you had listened: if you had only circled
back; if your bells and bewits had rattled like a rattlesnake's
tail dragging gravity behind it; if you'd let yourself be pinioned; if the blue
had not tempted you: unpeeling its skin like an apple snaking
off coil after coil; if it were true: that it's lucky to unwind the body of the sky
in a single piece; if the spiral had labyrinthed before the church
door and you had flown into its center like an angel turned back to the bird
it was before language confused feather and Father; if you had not
believed your wings unwritten pages—vast, wind-ruffled—
if you had let the hood come down like ordinary night and let your heart
take over; if you had heard it: rattling in the hollow inside you; if you had
circled it like a stupa, knowing you would not get closer,
but not getting farther

[I have had to learn the simplest things last. Which made for difficulties.]

Gulls of Cardiff, small gods of the unravel,
trash-blusterers, street screechers, chimney-pot clouds
sweeping yourselves away to sky
on grey days when all my luggage
for a year of living is still lost, and Bishop's *So many things*
seem filled with the intent is an escalator
looping up and up too steep for me to ride; repeating
one too-trim line for the scatterage
of garbage at the concrete stoop, the see-through dress
bought from the last shop closing when the train pulled in;
the fabric's feathers like pastel peacocks or some mythic bird
at the gateway of the land of *What Is Ours And Will Never Go Away*:
that empty lot
where the sign has rusted through and only you
keep landing, screaming *baguette, orange rind, fish,*
dragging the damp, lost innards of this world toward
beaky light—dragging the innards we don't want to see
because of whatever else we want
too much: Each next flat to be my home. Myself
to seem arranged (in my missing bra and missing skirt
and missing clip) (more fully wearing them without them
than I ever did). What sort of daemon
that, despite myself, I've always loved, that thinks instead
in storms and seasons, hatch of ants (whose acids
make you drunk, the papers say), that snatches sandwiches
mid-bite and dive-bombs cancer patients
wheeled to hospital lawns, not caring
what they've lost, lifting to sky whatever food you can:
more manna maybe than it ever was. For you, the city has hired
a hawk (named Jack) to circle City Hall, so you'll think he roosts
where, beautifully shameless, hordes of you call
more hordes to wade the cobbled slush. Unnamed. Or named
as *Scourge*, you split black plastic bags like mussels
outside every door I think could be (should be)

mine, then lose. *Where the garment gapes*, Barthes says,
is what seduces most. Harbingers of my childhood Gulf,
the mud flats, fish in oil tankers' wakes, your wings
indignantly alive as Yeats' desert birds, remind me now
I'm most alive when the world's intent and my intentions
angle so far off that hunger leaks, and the sea
swarms in, and I cannot say for certain
what should be mine to love.

Cambium

I have come to love the tree's story
        —Maureen Laflin, woodworker

When the myth was cut down, and the thick cedar
chain mail of its bark no longer held her,
they expected the woman would step into the clearing
grateful—something tentative as spring about her step; a knot softening
back into a bruise from where the god she'd run from
had caught her by the ankle to grasp her down into the moss
and curse of roots.

They wanted her to make kindling
of loneliness, or reveal it as a nest with a single, small blue egg.

In their myth of how the myth let her go, she would speak
like a rush of needles in the rain about her prison.

So when she took the saw into her hands instead,
what they imagined was revenge: her subtracting who she
was from unasked branches;

and when she planed one plank for a narrow table
what they imagined were the years she'd lived in fear,
which they hadn't seen; when she'd mythically disappeared—each ring
she could sand at last into fine, dead pollen.

In the myth (though this was never mentioned) there must
have been another life she'd lived
and could return to, as if after long, strange travel, knocking
on the door of someone simply human.

Once, the people said (and it was true), she had
knelt as a child by a river and skipped flat stones,
listening for the plink and ripple of her smooth, concentric futures.

[76]

It had all happened differently. But doesn't it?
Where the lines of the wood most arced and blurred,

wavering like the Milky Way inversely darkened, or a smudge
of freckles—she knew there had been branches:
wind-lofted, bird-
tufted, disbalancing. Where the lines had lengthened:
the quickened thickening that had held her, leaning, upright.

She rubbed teak oil along these; she rested
her elbows on them. *Reaction wood,*
this is called in science. *Living,*
this was called in the long green while
when it had happened to her.

In the Glass Labyrinth at the Nelson Atkins Art Museum, the Rough Beast is Mistaken for the Minotaur

As if a beast can enter, at will, any myth's
clear walls: as if each labyrinth promises anything
      but a nest for the egg of the self you've already
hatched. As if Plutarch didn't get there first. As if Paul Simon
      didn't get there after, "Mother and Child Reunion"
rhythming away in The Beast's earbuds, and the walls
      winding one way in, which is the same way back,
which is maybe what Aristotle meant by "infinite sequence"
      or Simon by "a motion away," which is where his face is
each time he looks for it: reflected in the lawns' reflection just
      ahead, like that joke on the Jungle Cruise (where a kid
called him "wildebeest") where the "pygmy" waves a shrunken head,
      and the guide cries, "What's that up there in the river
a-head?" Funny-not-funny mother of all mythologies:
      that the future will mirror the name we call it. The glass
Windexed so clear even here it looks like air he almost birds
      head-first into as the kid says "Look," gesturing finger-
horns like it's a zoo; like in this real labyrinth, you'd need
      a string. Though it's not the kid's fault the language of
myths got tangled so far back there is no unicursal path now:
      the past as uncertain as the future, as Diderot said.
Or as the Beast wants to say, "No, kid, I'm Superman,"
      miming bird-plane arms, though the corridors are
too narrow for wings or explanations like, *I'm walking toward*
      Bethlehem, which could as well mean *away from Bethlehem*
and back, or *I'm walking* until the end, which never comes,
      no single shell-crack, but more world sputtering on
in frying pans and oiled reggae licks and Chinese menus and
      squat bronze Henry Moores and gum-cheeked kids
pasting their faces to the glass like aquarium fish, all of it
      roped together in some great paradox science
explains now as mutation—a chicken hatches from an egg
      of another bird, and they both came first: what's that

a-head? The future! One beast or another—
   like the chalazae (suspending what will be and
the strange what-is) roping yolk to white to shell.

The Rough Beast Literally Arrives

and the birds of the earth have all been replaced
            by pixels. They are literally just specks of light
in the trees and hedges: a shine perching on car hoods
            in the indignant desert of the grocery store lot.
The Rough Beast arrives on a day that could be any day
            when the birds have all died and people are literally
crying at their screens and changing oil at Jiffy Lube and
            wheeling out shopping carts, oblivious, with Solo
cups colored like cardinals, if that color could ruffle
            and preen. And people are waking in the pitch-
corrected dark to harp-sound on cell phones, searching
            orioles and *warblers* they've only vaguely heard of
but love now; staring out windows where there would've

            been a birdhouse at literally any grandmother's,
where jays and small brown birds we didn't know or wonder
            names of would flock, and we'd sing to ourselves
our secret pop-song, *build a little birdhouse in your soul,*
            which didn't make literal sense—that canary that
was also a lightbulb somehow inside us, which was also
            literally how it felt then to be young in the world
of birds: glowing and fluttering out and in, like *Everyone in*
            me is a bird, and wasn't Sexton literally confessing
that she lived in a real body with too many wings crammed
            inside it? *Literally* meaning, originally, *to the letter,*
of literature, before people started saying it for literally
            everything. And birds too so ubiquitous once

we saw them as ourselves: the part prone to flock in high,
            struck trees, the part that only wanted a grandmother
to feed us at the edge of winter, the part that would startle,
            flapping homeward, though home's door is closed,
we hammered it drunkenly too small for our own flighty
            bodies once during a Christmas drinking game
when the bartender handed literal hammers to drunk people

to see who could build a birdhouse fastest from
a little board-and-nail pile, and we built one, didn't we?
Or the part we scared away with cannons blasting
on the campus lawns each fall so we literally couldn't
hear our professors or the invasive starlings
that I was geeky-glad to learn were imported by a man

who wanted to bring America each bird in
Shakespeare, as if Shakespeare were a place, as if birds
were decorations that wouldn't deafen us with
their overbreeding, their exodus and returning. Though
even the starlings are truly gone now, even
the sparrows with soft stock-footage plumage, even
finches bright as rainbow-winged angels from
Renaissance paintings, angels that, when the Rough Beast
arrives, literally 77% of Americans say they believe
in, the Biblical literalists calling everyone else *sneering factual*
literalists, so it's no wonder, an article tells me,
in this age of *relativistic hopscotch* and *spiraling subjectivities*—
this gyre of scrolling and rescrolling for meaning—

that everyone keeps saying *literally* because it's getting hard
to speak plainly or intensely enough. It's getting hard
to say how it feels to wake to pixels and the sky that in the past
50 years (literally 7.14% of time since the Renaissance)
has gone so blank those painters wouldn't recognize it:
the fresco plaster is too wet or too dry or too acid
for birds to stick to it, so we only have bleached-out angels
fluttering in space and the space-age shivelights of
skyscrapers reflecting steel public sculptures shaped like
phalluses or donuts that every city has now
instead of mud and marshland so there's literally nowhere
for birds to roost or for the Rough Beast to rest
his paws, though here he is. Here we are. Here we are.

NOTES ON THE POEMS

The Rough Beast of these poems has wandered out of William Butler Yeats' "The Second Coming."

"Correlations" cites, among other sources, "The Disturbing Sound of a Human Voice" by Ed Yong, graphs from the Spurious Correlations website, and John Ashbery's "The Ecclesiast."

"Crossed Letters" takes as its metaphoric form the 19th-century practice of crossed letters (or crosshatched letters): because postage and paper were so expensive, people would write one direction across the page, and then rotate the page and write over their words the other way (which is—as I learned at Trinity College in Dublin, where I first saw these—amazingly still readable).

"It is undone business I speak of, this morning" and "I have had to learn the simplest things last. Which made for difficulties" are lines from Charles Olson's "Maximus, to himself."

"No one would eat a Cezanne apple" is from Altieri's *The Art of Twentieth-Century American Poetry*.

In "Mean High Water," "Charm's in limited supply and refusing to stretch" is a line from Martin Gore's "Compulsion"; "There's no wind in this part of your voyage. I repeat: we are gyrating motionless" is from Eunice Odio's *The Fire's Journey* Part I, translated by Keith Ekiss with Sonia P. Ticas and Mauricio Espinoza; "I learned, later, that he was simply terrified, / And that a gang of boys had crept up, earlier, / With sticks—" is Larry Levis (also quoted in "Sad Clown Paintings.")

In "The Goth Comes Clean About Decay," "I pitied the bathtub its forced embrace of the human form" is a riff off a Matthea Harvey title that has rattled in my head for years.

In "The Rough Beast Literally Arrives," "Everyone in me is a bird" is a line by Anne Sexton that I've likewise been carrying around. The poem also owes a debt to, and quotes from, "Literally—the much misused word of the moment" by Ben Masters.